Only take heed to thyself, and keep thy soul diligently,
Lest thou forget the things which thine eyes have seen,
And lest they depart from thy heart all the days of thy life;
But teach them to thy sons and thy sons' sons . . .

—*Deuteronomy 4, 9*

This book is dedicated to Adrien, Élisabeth, Antoine, Pierre, Émile, Armand, and Théodore

Based on an idea by Diane Barbara. Designed by Diane Barbara and Dominique Beccaria.

This book is for grandmothers
and their grandchildren,
from the youngest to those
who have grown a little older.

This book is also for parents,
grandfathers, and grown-ups
of any relation.

It is for anyone who would like
to help a child learn more about
his or her grandmother!

A Ladder Through Time

Everyone has a mother and a father.
And we all have grandparents.
We have both a paternal grandmother and grandfather
(our father's parents),
and a maternal grandmother and grandfather
(our mother's parents).
Our grandparents also had parents.
Our grandparents' parents are our great-grandparents.
In fact, our lineage goes farther and farther back,
from great-great-grandparents to great-great-great-grandparents,
and so on. It is as though we are climbing a ladder that goes
farther and farther into the centuries of time.

As you and your grandmother fill in the pages of this book,
it will be as if the two of you are climbing
your very own ladder of time—together!

My Grandmother's Genealogy

Let's see now . . . who was my little cousin's great-great-great-grandfather?

A genealogist is a person who researches ancestors,
and ancestors are the people in your family
who came before you did.
We call what a genealogist does "genealogy."

A genealogist makes pages and pages of charts,
which show the names and birthdays of each member of a family.
Since these charts are easier to read when they are shaped like
trees, they are often called "family trees."

In the small boxes to
the left, starting with
yourself at the top,
write the names and
birth dates of each
member of your family.

By creating your own family tree, you are exploring the history
of where you and your grandmother came from.
You are discovering who your ancestors are
and in what ways you are related to one another.
If you can fill in all the boxes by yourself, good for you!
And if not, ask your grandmother to help you.
Either way, you will learn a whole lot about your own genealogy.

My Grandmother's Childhood
Her Birth

A new baby . . . now that's something very special! If your great-grandparents are still living, perhaps they can tell you about your grandmother's birth. But if not, then ask your grandmother herself.

Where was she born?
Was your great-grandfather there at her birth?
Did she have brothers and sisters waiting for her at home?

Tell me, Grandmother, did your parents hold any kind of religious ceremony for you after you were born?

If they did, what was it?_____
When did it happen?_____
Where was it?_____
Did you wear a special dress?
_____

Question Box

A short history of my grandmother's birth

In this circle, write what you now know about your grandmother's birth.

My Grandmother as a Baby

Just like you, your grandmother had to learn to eat, walk, talk, and do everything else children do.
Did she have a stroller? A nursery? A favorite toy?
Did she wear cloth or disposable diapers?
Back then, did baby food come in little jars like it does now?

Ask your grandmother if she has a photograph of herself as a baby. Paste it here if you can. Or make a photocopy and paste that here instead. Look closely at the picture. Notice how your grandmother is dressed. Is it different from how children are dressed now? Can you name the people who are with her? Use little arrows to show who is who!

My Grandmother's Parents,
My Great-grandparents

What were your grandmother's parents (your great-grandparents) like?
Were they strict? Were they funny?
Where did they like to go?
What did they like to do?
Do you look like either one of them?
After you paste their pictures below,
ask your grandmother to tell you what
she remembers about them.

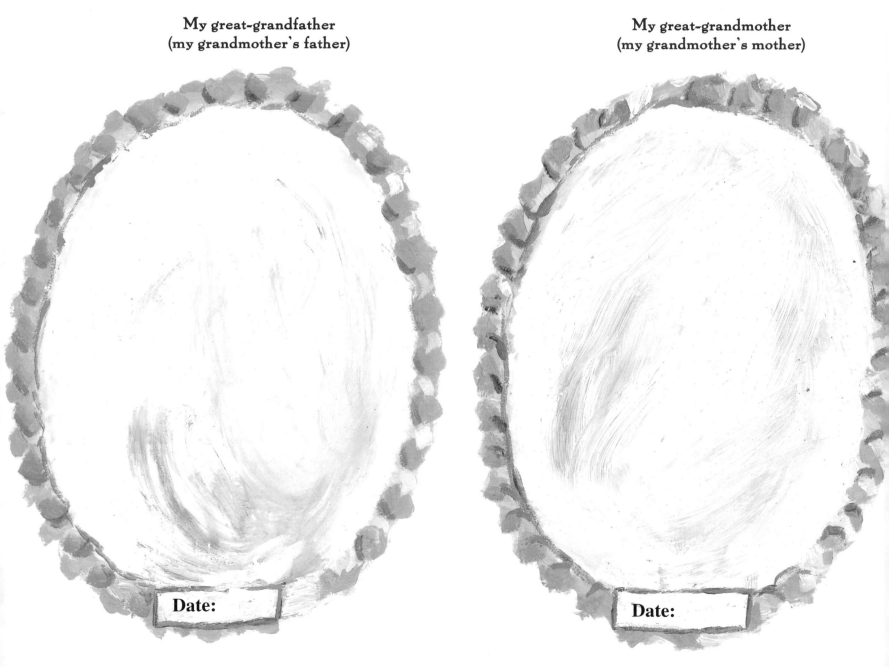

My great-grandfather
(my grandmother's father)

My great-grandmother
(my grandmother's mother)

Date:

Date:

My Grandmother as a Little Girl
Her Brothers, Sisters, and Friends

Perhaps your grandmother has brothers and sisters—if so, they are your great-uncles and great-aunts. Or perhaps she is an only child. If so, maybe she has cousins, and certainly she has friends with whom she got into mischief! Ask your grandmother about these people and write what she tells you below.

What are the names of her brothers and sisters? _____

_____

What number child is your grandmother in her family? _____

Who are the cousins she played with the most? _____

_____

And who, as a child, were her best friends? _____

What did she and her friends like to do together? _____

_____

Is there a song they liked to sing? _____

If so, ask your grandmother to teach it to you!

Did her family go on vacations together? If they did, where did they go? _____

Did your grandmother and her sisters and brothers go to the same school? Where was it? _____

_____

Is there anything else about her childhood that she wants you to know? _____

_____

_____

Her favorite toy

Her secret spot

Her silliest trick

Her sweetest memory

Her grades in school

Say, Grandmother, did you ever get a time-out?

Tell me, Grandmother, what color was your favorite dress?

Question Box

*Record your grandmother's memories
in any way you wish—with
drawings, in words, or with photographs or photocopies.*

Her House

Do you know where your grandmother lived as a child?
Was it in the city or in the country? Was it inland or by the ocean?
Did she live in a house or in an apartment?
Did she ever have to move?

Ask her to give you more details. How did her family
heat their house? Did she have her own room?
Did they have any pets?
And did anyone else live there with them?

Paste a photograph of your grandmother's childhood home here.

A Teenager, Then a Young Woman...

Fifteen, eighteen, twenty, then twenty-five years old . . . Your grandmother grew up, and as she did, she created her life's path: She made friends, she found a job, she pursued her hobbies, she met your grandfather, and so much else.

How interesting to discover more about your grandmother as a young woman. Just think, back then, she may have had no idea that she would have children, and after that, even grandchildren!

Date:

Paste a photograph here of your grandmother as a young woman. What was in fashion back then?

How My Grandmother and Grandfather Met

You are the way you are today, with your distinctive eyes and hair, with your particular mom and dad, because one day, your grandfather and grandmother met. Ask each of them to tell you about their first meeting.

BE CAREFUL! GRANDFATHERS ARE SOMETIMES TEMPTED TO COPY!

We met on _____
at _____
The weather was _____
I was wearing _____
_____
Your grandfather was wearing _____
_____
He said _____
_____
I said _____
_____
I have to add that _____
_____

Grandmother's version

We met on _____
at _____
The weather was _____
I was wearing _____
_____
Your grandmother was wearing _____
_____
She said _____
_____
I said _____
_____
I have to add that _____
_____

Grandfather's version

Ask your grandparents to tell you how they met. Have them answer the questions above on two separate, carefully prepared sheets of paper. Then copy what they've written here and read their answers together!

My Grandmother As a Young Mother

Imagine your grandmother as a young mother,
with one or more children!
Like your mom, sometimes she is happy, other times she is anxious.
She's an energetic mom who takes care of her family, keeps her house in order,
and who maybe even has another job besides.

Imagine if your grandmother's life were a movie . . .

**A short movie about my grandmother's life
as a young mother**

*Draw, write,
and/or paste
pictures here
to create a
"movie."*

The silliest thing my mom or dad ever
did as a child

How my grandmother got ready for
Christmas or Hanukkah

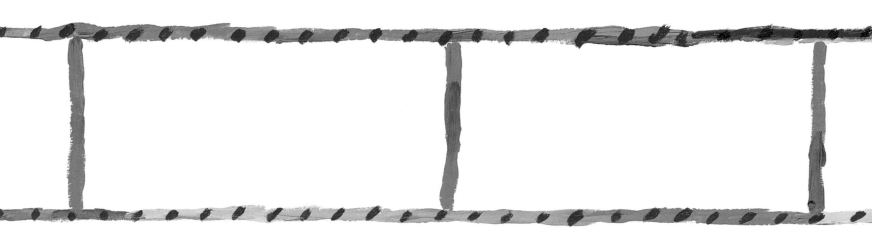

My grandmother raising her children

And here's my grandfather, too, helping
her with their children!

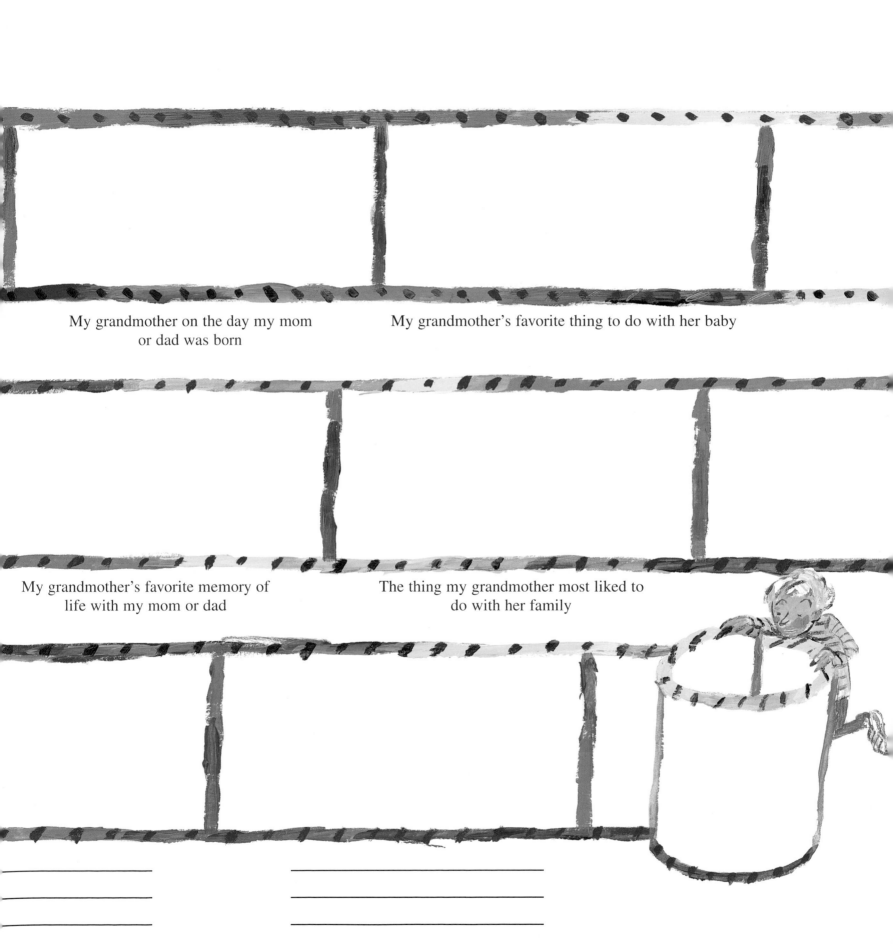

My grandmother on the day my mom
or dad was born

My grandmother's favorite thing to do with her baby

My grandmother's favorite memory of
life with my mom or dad

The thing my grandmother most liked to
do with her family

_____

_____

_____

_____

Grandmother, how did you and Grandfather choose my mom or dad's first name?

_____
_____
_____

Tell me, Grandmother, what was my mom or dad like at my age?

_____
_____

Grandmother, what food did my mom or dad like the most?

_____

Question Box

Grandmother, did my mom or dad do well in school?

_____
_____

A letter or drawing done by my mom or dad as a child

In this space, paste a photocopy (or original) letter or drawing
that your mom or dad did as a child and that
your grandmother has kept all these years!
If she doesn't have one, paste a
favorite picture she has of your mom or dad as a little kid here instead.

My Grandmother and Her Work

Perhaps your grandmother worked, and maybe still works,
outside her home. If not, then most likely her job was
and still is to take care of her family and her house.
She probably also has always had hobbies she pursues,
such as a sport, gardening, painting, or sewing.
Ask her to tell you about her jobs and her hobbies.

The Journey of Life

Life is like a journey along a path.
Sometimes the path is straight,
without any curves or bends,
and sometimes it meanders and winds all around.

Often there are obstacles to cross and turns to make, but there are also places
where you can stop, look, and simply enjoy the view!

Like everyone else, your grandmother is traveling along her own path.

Kites Are Like Signs in the Sky

With your grandmother, as with any human being you love,
you have bonds. These bonds are like kite strings,
strong and resistant.
Because they are in place, you can soar and fly,
knowing they are there, connecting you to something
sure and true.

She has time
spend with m

She plays with me.

She's there when
things are bad.

We play cards
together.

We read books
together.

She thinks of me.

She is gentle.

I spend vacations with her.

She listens to me.

She helps me with my homework.

I can call her when I need to.

She thinks I'm great.

I can tell her everything.

She smells good.

She loves to take care of me.

She teaches me what she knows.

She tells me stories from the past.

e tucks me in t night.

She makes me delicious things to eat.

When I'm with her, I can do what I love to do.

e explains gs to me.

A Gift

In and of itself, this book is a gift.
For in completing it together, you and your grandmother
have given a lot of time and attention to each other . . .

Now the time has come for each of you to create a special
letter, poem, or drawing for the other . . .
Put whatever you make into this envelope, so that you will
always have a token of how much you love and mean to
each other.